GREAT FUGUES
for Solo Keyboard

Edited by
DAVID DUTKANICZ

DOVER PUBLICATIONS, INC.
Mineola, New York

DEDICATION

To Evdokia and Boris
"Vyechnaya Pamyat"

Bibliographical Note

Great Fugues for Solo Keyboard, first published in 2007, is a new compilation
of works reproduced from early authoritative editions.

International Standard Book Number: 0-486-45727-3

Manufactured in the United States of America
Dover Publications, Inc., 31 East 2nd Street, Mineola, N.Y. 11501

Contents

Fugue in G Minor

GIROLAMO FRESCOBALDI

The Cat's Fugue

Domenico Scarlatti

One day the favorite cat of Scarlatti walked over the keyboard producing by chance the following notes: which the master used as the theme for a Fugue.

Fugue in E Minor

PADRE MARTINI GIAMBATTISTA

Fugue in G Major

G. 231

GEORGE FRIDERIC HANDEL

Fugue in G Minor
G. 264

George Frideric Handel

Fugue No. 1
from WTC Book I

JOHANN SEBASTIAN BACH

Fugue No. 2
from WTC Book I

JOHANN SEBASTIAN BACH

Fugue No.6
from WTC Book I

Johann Sebastian Bach

Fugue No. 16
from WTC Book I

JOHANN SEBASTIAN BACH

Fugue No. 7
from WTC Book II

JOHANN SEBASTIAN BACH

Fugue No. 14
from WTC Book II

JOHANN SEBASTIAN BACH

Moderato ♩ = 72 (Tovey: similar)

a 3.

Fugue No. 15
from WTC Book II

JOHANN SEBASTIAN BACH

Fugue No. 24
from WTC Book II

JOHANN SEBASTIAN BACH

34

St. Anne's Fugue

from Prelude and Fugue, BWV 552

Transcribed by F. Busoni

Johann Sebastian Bach

Allegro risoluto ed energico.

marc.

Fugue No. 1
from Art of the Fugue

Johann Sebastian Bach

Fugue No. 7

from Art of the Fugue

JOHANN SEBASTIAN BACH

46

Fugue in A Major
on a Theme of Albinoni, BWV 950

JOHANN SEBASTIAN BACH

Fugue in C Major
from The Clavier-Büchen of W. F. Bach, BWV 953

JOHANN SEBASTIAN BACH

Fugue in Bb Major
arranged from J. A. Reincken's Hortus Musicus, BWV 954

JOHANN SEBASTIAN BACH

55

Variation No. 10
from Goldberg Variations

JOHANN SEBASTIAN BACH

Fugue
from Chromatic Fantasy and Fugue, BWV 903

JOHANN SEBASTIAN BACH

Fugue

from Fantasia and Fugue in C Major, K. 394

WOLFGANG AMADEUS MOZART

Andante maestoso.

Fugue in G Minor
K. 154

Wolfgang Amadeus Mozart

(Sechter.)

Finale
from Eroica Variations

LUDWIG VAN BEETHOVEN

Fugue No. 1

from Six Preludes and Fugues, Op. 35

FELIX MENDELSSOHN

Choral.

sempre forte e tenuto

do con forza

il Basso dim.

piano e stacc.

p e tranquillo

dolce

Andante come prima

Fugue No. 6

from Six Preludes and Fugues, Op. 35

FELIX MENDELSSOHN

Fugue No. 1
from Seven Pieces in Fugal Form, Op. 126

Robert Schumann

Fugue No. 2

from Seven Pieces in Fugal Form, Op. 126

ROBERT SCHUMANN

*This page has been left intentionally blank
in order to facilitate page turns*

Fugue No. 6

from Seven Pieces in Fugal Form, Op. 126

ROBERT SCHUMANN

Fugue No. 1
from 3 Preludes and Fugues, Op. 16

Clara Schumann

Allegro vivace.

Fugue

from Variations and Fugue on a
Theme of Handel, Op. 24

JOHANNES BRAHMS

Etude No. 3 – Fugue
from Six Etudes, Op. 52

Camille Saint-Saëns

Etude No. 2, *Alla Fuga*

from Six Etudes for the Left Hand, Op. 135

CAMILLE SAINT-SAËNS